Nature

is unlimited broadcasting station:
Flowers she wore on her feet.

Let us keep walking, wearing beautiful flowers on our feet.
There are always flowers for those who want to see them.

An Autobiography

NEEMA EDWARD MKWELELE

By Bertha Mkwelele and Edward Mkwelele.

Tellwell Talent
www.tellwell.ca

ISBN
978-0-2288-1117-6 (Hardcover)
978-0-2288-1116-9 (Paperback)
978-0-2288-1118-3 (eBook)

Nature

is unlimited broadcasting station:
Flowers she wore on her feet.

The story of Neema Edward Mkwelele

An autobiography

BERTHA MKWELELE AND EDWARD MKWELELE.

To Neema, first and foremost, who hadn't asked us to dedicate a book to her. This wasn't the one we had in mind. We never dreamt of writing a book anyway. But this one's for you, Neema. For the lessons you taught us, the gifts that you gave us, the heart that you gave us and all the love that we shared. Remarkable and beautiful memories, wider than the ocean and bigger than the sky.

Keep smiling Neema, and fly well, our beautiful daughter, until we meet again.

With all our Love. Mom and Daddy.

To Neema and Michael

for all they have given us:

a hunger to learn,

the joy of travel,

the ability to laugh at ourselves, and with each other.

To all people who cared so much about her, rejoiced for her, laughed with her, cried for her. To all those who worked so hard to make her life as thrilling as it was. To all the people who were there for her and those who made a difference in her short life. And to members of our extended family, Bertha's side and Edward's side and the best brothers and sisters in the world, you are the most precious gifts of our life, just as Neema was, and is, and always will be. For the love and strength and laughter that we share, that you gave Neema, and that she gave us. May you be forever blessed, and may you never again know a sorrow and loss like this one.

With all our love,

Bertha and Edward.

Important regions (countries) in Neema's Life

1. Dar-es-salaam, Tanzania

2. Kenya

3. Falmouth, United Kingdom

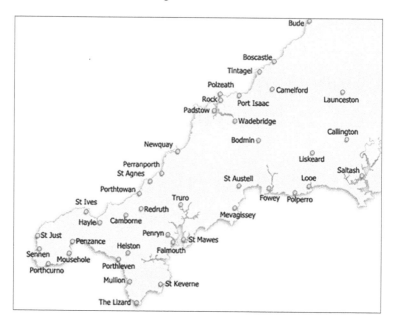

3. Vancouver, Canada

4. Santiago, Chile

Prologue

This will not be an easy book to write, but there is much to say, in our own words and our daughter's. And as hard as it may be to write, it's worth doing it, if it helps inspire girls in Tanzania as well as the African continent and around the world.

It is hard to encapsulate a being, a very special one—a soul, a smile, a laugh, a girl, a huge talent, an enormous heart, a child, a young woman—in however many pages. Yet, we must try, for her, ourselves, for other girls. And we hope that as we do, you will come to understand who she was, and what she meant to all those who knew her.

This is the story of an extraordinary girl and young woman with a brilliant mind, a heart of gold, who is gone too soon. It has been seven years since we lost our beautiful only daughter and our first child, Neema, as we write this book. We still cry at the sound of her name. Our hearts still ache and will forever ache. It is still impossible to absorb or understand, and harder still to accept. We look at her photographs and cannot imagine that all that life and love and energy has vanished.

The purpose of this book is to pay tribute to her, and to write what she accomplished in her short life. Neema was an extraordinary young woman, with joy and wisdom, and with a remarkably profound, great understanding about herself and others. She faced life with courage and passion and humour. She would agree with us that this book is about Neema. The book we're writing is about telling the world what kind of girl she was, and at the same time telling the world about those things she fell in love with, those things she loved and was happy doing. Neema's personal core values were what she lived by: making life truly amazing for herself. She valued fun, and authenticated happiness as the greatest value in her life.

We're writing this book to honour our first child and only beautiful daughter, and to remember her. But there is yet another purpose in writing this book. We want to share the story and the pain, the courage, the love, and what we learned in living through it. More important to us is that there is much to learn here, not only about one life, but the legacy Neema left behind and its impact on other people around the world, including children and young people, especially girls and young women.

If it's true that we're going to transform girls' lives around the world, we need everyone to join us. Then girls can be helped, get all the support needed, and get a better education to realize their potential, regardless of their backgrounds. And if possible, we would love to share Neema's story, Neema's life, to help encourage girls to follow her footsteps. We're telling this story of Neema's life to inspire them, perhaps help them to learn from Neema's accomplishments and her victories, and to do more beyond Neema's accomplishments.

Yes, we miss our first child and our only beautiful daughter so dearly. There was nothing better in life than knowing that things were going well with her. As a happy young woman, Neema just graduated with her BA (Hons) in broadcasting from the University of Falmouth in the United Kingdom, and she was preparing herself to go to Chile in South America. Neema fell in love with South American people and their culture; she met them at Emily Carr University in Vancouver, Canada. Neema enjoyed her time in Vancouver when she was doing an international exchange program. She spoke about this experience honestly and always referred to it as her "great travelling experience," and enjoyed everything about it. After finishing her program at Emily Carr, Neema went back to the United Kingdom to continue her studies at the University of Falmouth.

She went back with her mind set, and she made it clear to us and everyone in her life circle that she would one day travel to one of those South American countries. She wanted to go there to live, work, and become a travel writer. She was determined and nothing could have possibly stopped her. Neema got her- self an internship program with a German the tourism company, Chile Inside. Chile Inside operates in the Pacific Ocean, in Santiago, the capital city of Chile.

Neema was a priceless gift to us. She taught us everything worth knowing about life and love, everything about what it means to be a best friend. May God bless and keep her, and cuddle her, until we meet her again.

Bertha and Edward.

Chapter One

INTRODUCTION

Neema was born on the firth day of January 1989 in Tanzania. She was the first child of Bertha and Edward, and was the only beautiful daughter of the family. She was given a gorgeous name on Earth, and Neema really loved her name because to her the name meant so many nice things. She was aware that Neema is a Swahili name meaning "grace" in English. She lived in Tanzania as a child and attended primary school and secondary school in Kenya. Neema lived with her mother, father, and her young brother, Michael.

Strange, Neema, what did you say? That is what Neema would be saying today as we write this book for her and about her. That's right, strange. As a girl of seven years old, Neema would come home from school, sit on the sofa and read newspapers. Yes, that's Neema, and here we mean that was *our* Neema. She was a strange person in a good way in the world. She liked reading and had fallen in love with it since she was a little girl. Reading, among other things, shaped Neema's personality, her beliefs and values, and her career choice as well. More importantly, we would like to say here that Neema liked to read, and reading was her way of having fun, too.

Here above is Neema at the age of 7 years, reading a newspaper at her parents' house in Mbezi Beach area, Dar-es-salaam, Tanzania. Michael, Neema's young brother, is standing behind her and just wondering what to do next—should he join his sister to read the newspapers or should he just go and do something else instead?

This is what Neema would do, and in this way she educated herself and equipped herself with the knowledge of a lot of things as she grew up to know her surroundings and the world…is there a world? Yes, while most girls of her age were out playing, what would Neema have been doing inside the house? When her friends went out Neema would sit on the sofa and read magazines, newspapers, and books.

She would also watch TV, sit on the computer, and do a little bit of music. Now let's get to the point: Neema was a little girl, our first child, and a child like any other, and of course she went out to play like any child or did all the things that children do.

Neema.

She was a little bit shy—she was confident, but shy. Yes, that's right. More seriously, her family and friends would describe her as easygoing, a good listener, a word-player and an extraordinary person who nicknamed herself "unbroken-divine." Neema was the kind of girl who would go out and grab the world by the lapels. She grew up having her mind set, and believed that you alone are enough. You have nothing to prove to anybody.

Neema would hope to laugh as much as I cry, to get her work done and try to love everyone and have the courage to accept the love in return. We believe that Neema would have been able to tell us what she feels about the world today. She would say, "I feel very hopeful, very expectant. I'm looking forward to it."

Life to Neema meant family and friends who
she would trust as they trusted her.

Beautifully, as the only daughter in the family, Neema got all the attention and grew up to impress core values she created herself. She was pretty much on the happy side of life, carrying a positive attitude as much as she could. She was always using her favourite saying: "This is what I am happy doing," but like all children and teenagers Neema had her own "days of." That means she had some sad days or frustrated days or depressed days. Neema would run to her mom and daddy and talk to them because she was close with them. They were affectionate. She also had few friends at home during school holidays and at school during school time. She was quick to reach out to her friends and talk to them as well. She made her school term as enjoyable as she possibly could, and thought of the next time she would go home for school holidays.

Neema grew up to become a young woman, completed primary school and secondary school and graduated with her first degree at the age of 21 years old. She was not seeing anyone in particular at primary school and secondary school, and here we mean that Neema herself would have called that moment "now," but she believed they were, and would call them, "school boyfriends." She would go out and tell her friends about favourite places she would like to go with her boyfriend. When Neema went to university she started getting serious, and had a serious relationship—she had a real boyfriend.

Neema's outlook for the future was something about this book. In the year of 2011, Neema was 22 years old, only a few months after finishing her first degree at the age of 21 years old. She was a graduate student and a young woman with a BA (Hons), ready to take on the world. She was preparing herself to go to Chile, one of the South American countries, for an internship program offered by Chile Inside, a tourism company based in Germany. She was a keen traveller and having just graduated in broadcasting, she was looking forward to gaining personal as well as professional experience as a researcher and becoming a writer for tourism and travel magazines. She was passionate about travelling and meeting people from different cultures. She was also passionate about writing and would have liked to combine the two likes together. She made her decision and chose Chile to live and work. She was quite confident that she would have worked hard, enjoyed sharing the life and culture as well as contributing to the people she lived with in Chile and elsewhere in the world. She would probably have married and had a family and children.

Neema was not the only member of her generation whose aspirations and subsequent career choice were shaped by both the traditional way, including reading, and the modern way, including new technology such as television. What was so special about Neema's future outlook? She was equipped and determined to make the most of her experience and contribute to the world in a unique way. She was ready and clearly presented herself as an individual and showed the world that she was happy and loved what she was doing.

She decided to walk with her career, using the career she adored and broadcasting what she loved doing, and broadcasting her love of nature and wearing flowers on her feet. She was born a natural leader, taking the lead to do something she profoundly believed in was very simple to her, because she was a happy girl who always strived to be happy at any cost. She would have gone on to educate people and contribute to the world, and these were the physical ingredients of her existence as we came to know it, and we gained insight into the understanding that was Neema's powerful message to all people around the world: that you can possibly educate others by doing simple things in life, change their way of thinking, inspire them and let them follow you and encourage them to work at having fun and be happy by putting smiles on their faces. On top of that, Neema would have said that her way was the simplest way to make their lives better and make a difference, no matter how small the difference in other people's lives.

Significantly, Neema believed that the world would have been much better if all people would have gone out and decided to keep walking, searching for beautiful flowers, wearing those beautiful flowers on their feet in their own individual style because there are always flowers for those who want to see them. More precisely, she would have said that the world would have been much better if all people would have gone out and decided to do simple things to make differences in other people's lives.

Keep walking and keep smiling, because life is a
beautiful thing and there's so much to smile about.

Chapter Two

1989-1995

Neema was our only child for more than four years. She enjoyed all the attention from her parents from 1989 to 1993. Her younger brother Michael was born in September 1993, about four years and nine months after Neema was born. So, Neema was a little bit bigger when her young brother came to the world. She was spoiled a little bit because of being alone and getting all the attention she wanted from both of her parents. Although Neema was the only child and a spoiled one, she had a big heart and she was big enough to understand what was going on around her in her own world at that particular time.

Neema was very happy the day we brought little Michael home from hospital. She demonstrated her sense of humour at a very young age and we are happy to share this experience with the whole world. As parents we're thrilled and as we write this book, we would like to tell the world that we are proud of her, we have been proud of her since, and we will continue to be proud of her forever. This is what our young girl Neema did on that day: she went to sit next to her mother, and asked questions about the baby boy her mom had brought home with her. She admired the baby boy, Michael, and she was not shy in showing love and affection right away for the human being lying down in front of her.

It's so beautiful to remember that the young Neema was happy to have her new sibling as part of her life, and she decided to start her new life on that day by inviting the newborn Michael into her life in her own unique way. She took her parents by surprise. Neema went to her bedroom and brought some clothes with her, and then she said, "These clothes don't fit me anymore," and looked at her father first and then looked at her mom and said, "I would like my brother to have them." She also asked a question of her mother, "Mom, can you dress him please?" We both had a good laugh, and Neema insisted that we make Michael try those clothes. We thanked our little girl Neema for being kind to her little brother, new baby-boy Michael.

As we looked at our little girl Neema enjoying her new life experience, we remembered what Neema had told us about one year before Michael was born. It was one of those beautiful days, when our little girl Neema would go out to play with our neighbours' children. So, on that day, Neema came to us crying and when she was asked what was happening and what was wrong, Neema did not answer right away.

And then she just answered us by saying, "Them, Mom," and she continue to cry and say, "I like to play with them, Mom, but—" and she did not finish what she wanted to say. Then when I asked her to stop crying, to calm down and tell what happened, and I pushed a little bit more about our neighbours' two boys who Neema enjoyed playing with (we asked, "What about them?") Neema wiped her tears and answered, "They laugh at me because I have no one at home to play with." We comforted her and told her that yes, we agreed that at that particular time she had no one to play with at home because she was the only child. We carefully chose what to say and explained to her that one day things would change. We would get a second child and therefore one day she will get someone to play with at home, and we will get a baby girl so she will have a sister to play with at home, or we will get a baby boy so she will get a little brother to play with.

We continued to say that we were proud of our beautiful daughter Neema from a very young age, because she was not shy about showing her vulnerability and always asked for help. On that day we spoke with our little girl, who was young, just over four years old, with love and sense of humour like an adult, and we asked her to be patient because we would make it happen, although we did not know when. Neema wiped up her tears again, and said, "I am going back to play with them, and I will tell them what you just told me." She went back to play with the two boys and told them that one day she would get a little sister or a little brother to play with her at home. We just reminded her to enjoy and have a lot of fun and come home early. Incredibly, this is one of the many beautiful memories we're celebrating and continue to celebrate and share with the world, because our little Neema did not stop doing what was making her happy at that particular time, and it did not matter what other children said to her, or if something was said to upset her. We enjoyed this attitude and continued to enjoy

Neema's positive attitude and behaviour as she continued to grow up.

It was amazing to watch our little girl Neema growing up to become a young confident person and young woman. Neema loved nature and everything around nature since the time she was able to understand what was going around her. We saw this and we saw what was happening to our little girl and stood by her and supported and guided her properly. We're thrilled as we write this book and share our parenting experience, our parenting story, including our motherhood and our fatherhood, and we're happy to say that it's awesome to say that we are proud about our daughter and we continue to be proud of her because she grew up to become the person we dreamed about. What kind of person would she have been, and what kind of a woman would she have been to this world during her short lifetime? One thing we're sure to talk about is that we watched and observed Neema many times, and we saw her showing her love for nature. She did that at all levels of her life circle, when she was at home and/or playing with other children around the house, when she was at school and when she was out and about enjoying other activities.

We liked and enjoyed everything, and, more important to us as parents, is that we enjoyed the way Neema connected herself with not only her own parents and other human beings on the earth, including her own young brother Michael, but the way she connected herself with nature. We continue to share with the world that it is more important to us to open up about these beautiful memories. More important to us is that the memories about our beautiful young daughter Neema as well as beautiful parenting memories are the reason that we would like to tell this to the world. Neema was an educated person and a young woman, who would go out and educate other children about her knowledge of everything, especially her love for nature. She would do that when playing with her friends and other children. She was also happy to take the lead in any activity she was involved with, and asked others to follow her, and she did that willingly and with great enthusiasm, and she would then tell or show her parents directly, without fear. For example, when she was around the house she would volunteer to water the plants in our house garden.

Neema watering plants at her parents' house garden.

Neema would talk about her experience, about her love of nature when she was busy watering the plants until the job was done. She would now and then tell her parents that she was going to tell other children and friends as well about what she had experienced at home and what she was excited about. When asked what she was going to tell them, Neema would just say, "I watered the plants today in my parents' house garden and enjoyed doing it because I love those plants and flowers. I would also tell them that I watched television and enjoyed those cartoons, human beings and animals playing in a beautiful garden."

She would also continue to talk about her love for nature, bringing up those things she enjoyed doing herself, and watching others do physically or on the television, and it was all about the love of nature. She would also tell her parents about flowers in the school garden and how her and her friend enjoyed them.

Chapter Three

1 9 9 5 - 2 0 0 2

Neema was enrolled in primary school in Kenya. We took Neema to take an entry test prior to enrollment because it was one of the requirements of the Kenyan government. The ministry of education in Kenya at primary-school level expected all private primary schools to cooperate and ask foreign students and their parents or guardians to comply. So we complied, and Neema did her entry test at the school and passed the test. She was happy when the results were announced to her and she went to her mother's ear and whispered, "I passed, Mom." We were both happy for her because she was cleared, meaning she was allowed to enrol and start schooling in Kenya. We took Neema home with us and waited for the opening day and then we brought her back to school.

Neema enjoyed travelling to school and coming back home. We also enjoyed taking our Neema to Kenya for schooling because travelling was something we loved doing, and travelling fit well into our hobbies and interests. Both of us loved travelling and travelling was in our blood. At a very young age and by the time she was literate, she saw and watched her parents enjoying the love of travelling. We would take Neema to school in Kenya every school season, at the beginning of every school term. Then, we would go and pick her up and bring her home at the end of every school term.

Neema loved it and we loved it because it was one of the life experiences by itself, and more important to us was that we were so happy to see our little Neema joining the club. We made a good number of trips back and forth, and then with time Neema thought about the idea of other students who would go home and get picked up at the border by the school bus. The school Neema went to had made a special arrangement, asking parents who lived closer to the Tanzania and Kenya border to get their children at the border. And then one day Neema asked permission to go on the school bus with other students.

She told us that she has been watching other students take the school bus and told us that she too wanted to see and experience how different it would be to go on the school bus with fellow students instead of being picked up directly from school. Later on in our life, as we continued to learn more from Neema, we would come to understand that Neema wanted to do something differently, and enjoy different experiences by riding a bus with her schoolmates as well as travelling home in the company of her schoolmates. We listened to Neema carefully and loved her more because of what she was, and we enjoyed watching her pick up her strength and courage from a very young age and approach us without fear.

After careful consideration, we declined permission. We explained to our little girl that we did not mind at all allowing Neema to join other students on the school bus, but the only excuse we had at that particular time was one thing, our only challenge, and we told Neema about it. We explained that we lived in Dar-es-salaam, and therefore Dar-es-salaam was too far away from the Tanzania–Kenya border. All in all, and in one way or another, we would have to come to Kenya anyway and bring Neema home.

It was an interesting subject to talk about. Neema asked us a lot of questions and we did our best to answer them all using simple language and examples for Neema to understand. We told her about the difference between her and other students who lived closer to the border. Parents of those students who live closer to the border are not in the situation of travelling from Dar-es-salaam to the border the same way we did. In the end we made a deal with her and promised Neema that we would let her try one or two trips and then the two of us would come to pick her up at the border. Neema was happy about this deal and agreed with us, and hoped that the next time she was coming home she would take the school bus together with her schoolmates, and we would have to travel up to the border instead of going directly to her school. She was so excited, and could not wait for that time to happen.

We were working parents, two of us working full time in the financial industry in Dar-es-salaam, Tanzania. We had very tight schedules, as well as challenges in terms of what we could do in terms of time. Luckily, and to our own advantage, the school arrangement was to let the students go home on weekends (Saturday and Sunday). We were working Monday to Friday, and therefore the school flexibility matched well with our needs and we enjoyed them, agreeing to receive students on weekends. We were happy with these arrangements because they fit exactly into our working lifestyle. Neema was too young to understand these challenges, and we believed that with time Neema would come to learn that we were working parents and that our choices were very limited in terms of time, and that going to pick her up directly from school was saving us a lot of time.

As we promised her, we gave Neema one chance to go on a school bus with other students. We planned well in advance and we did it during our vacation because we had all the time on Earth for anything unexpected. We asked the school to include Neema and let her take a ride with the other students, and the school bus would bring Neema to the border with them. We travelled and went to stay at the border for two days and then we headed back home to Dar-es-salaam. It was a different experience for Neema and for both of us. Neema enjoyed that experience; she had a lot to tell us: her friends at home in Dar-es-salaam, her friends at school as well as her teachers at her school. We really enjoyed travelling back home and listening to Neema tell us about her trip on a school bus. It was all beautiful and exciting, and there was lots of laughing all the way home.

We created a lifestyle around her, a little girl growing and developing very fast in all areas. Slowly, we could see ourselves passing on our love for travelling to our little Neema. Initially Neema was going to school alone and would come home to tell her little brother about her exciting experiences. We could see the two of them playing and talking about school and travelling, and in particular we saw Michael's curiosity clearly. He was curious about school-life experiences and especially schooling in a different country. This was the time Michael was still going to kindergarten school.

Then, little Michael would say to his sister that "the day will come when I will be coming to school with you." He also told his sister that he enjoyed what he was hearing from her about going to school in a different country. From time to time, he would come with us and ask us a lot of questions, and he would also ask when we would be taking him to school with his sister Neema. Michael was happy when he was told the time would come soon for him to go to school with his sister Neema. We explained to him that the right time would come when he was big enough to come out of kindergarten and go to school with his sister Neema. This is when we remembered Neema as a little girl, and this experience took us back to when we saw Neema start to show us her love for nature at a very young age, and by that time she was literate. We remain hopeful that the day will come when we see Michael doing the same as his sister, and maybe more than that.

The right time came, and Michael became a big boy, big enough to enroll in and start primary school. Michael was taken to do an entry test the same way Neema did. Michael passed the entry test and he was allowed to enroll and started schooling in Kenya. Now, we had both Neema and Michael going to school, and both went to the same school in Kenya. We both enjoyed travelling to Kenya to bring Neema and Michael to school and pick them up. We found ourselves bringing a little Michael into our world along with our love for travelling, and therefore four of us together walked with this love and enjoyed travelling to our neighbouring country, Kenya. As we continued to parent and enjoy our two children, making the most of this unique experience and having lots of fun and challenges, we were grateful that we did it that way and continued to stay on top of the education plan we had created for Neema and Michael.

It is interesting to say that we found ourselves falling deep into this thing of travelling, and it became a family thing and family interest. Four of us, father, mother, daughter and son began to love and enjoy travelling. Although by then, at that particular time, we were just travelling between the two countries, Kenya and Tanzania. We loved every moment and passed them on and shared them among us, two of us as parents and our two children, Neema and Michael. More important to us as parents was that we enjoyed watching our two children learning to love each other and take care of each other and accept their differences.

Neema and Michael went to the same primary school in Kenya. They both loved and enjoyed everything about school life. They would come home to tell us about the school life, their friends at school, their classmates, their teachers, their works, and they would always finish by saying that "it was fun." Then, they would always say they were looking forward to going back to school again. Neema was very kind to her little brother Michael. She loved him, supported him and protected him. It was who Neema was, a kind person, and she was a natural leader and not shy about taking the lead to guide and help her brother, not only at home, but she did the same thing when they went to school. Neema would show Michael how to pack his travelling bag better. When they did not agree on something, the two of them would work it out between themselves and resolve their differences amicably. Occasionally they would come to us and ask us to help them, and we enjoyed taking over and helping them resolve problems the two of them had experienced, especially at home.

Neema and Michael become closer to each other; they did their best to be there for each other and above all they became more than a sister and a brother. They became best friends. The two of them were inseparable, and we enjoyed watching our two children grow up and bond together. Michael had the advantage because he had his sister looking after him and supporting him in all his life issues, from home to school.

At the primary-school-education level in Kenya, the system states that students are required to complete and graduate after they finish their standard eight. Then came the time for Neema to complete and graduate after finishing standard eight at primary school level and move on to secondary school, so Neema was one among the students to do that.

After completing standard eight, Neema came home to wait for her final results. According to the ministry of education in Kenya, they put clear guidelines on allowing all students from private primary schools regardless of their nationalities to join national schools at the secondary-school level after passing their final standard eight examinations. And the national examination regulatory body set specific standards to meet that requirement. The ministry of education in Kenya set the pass mark as entry to national secondary schools, meaning all students are required to pass and get those marks in order to qualify for entry into national secondary schools, and therefore they would be selected to join national secondary schools regardless of their nationalities and regardless of whether students come from private primary schools or government primary schools. So, Neema did well and passed her standard eight final examinations, and she was cleared to enter national secondary school in Kenya from her private primary school in Kenya, even though she was not a Kenyan.

In 2003, Neema was enrolled in one of the top prestigious national secondary schools in Kenya. She was thrilled because she made her own history, and therefore lived to see her dreams come true. She was one of the few girls who worked hard and was very determined to reach the highest level. More important to Neema herself was that she was the only girl from her school selected to join other girls from all over Kenya to enroll at the national secondary school level. We set very high education standards for our two children and they too set their own standards. As parents we celebrated our daughter's achievement and we were happy to see that Neema was one of the few girls from private primary schools in Kenya to be selected to enter one of the number-one categories of national secondary schools in the country. We watched and enjoyed Neema. Michael also joined us, and the three of us joined her in celebrating together and discussing Neema passing her standard eight final examinations. And what did it mean to Michael himself? The four of us looked forward to seeing Neema walking to the next chapter of her life, and we promised to continue supporting her, and we welcomed the new experience and its challenges. We also told Michael that we looked forward to seeing him following in his sister's footsteps.

The three of us congratulated Neema, and we had family friends, school friends, school teachers and neighbours also congratulating her. It was a wonderful moment in our lifetimes, and by doing this Neema added one of the beautiful memories she would leave behind for us to remember and continue to celebrate her short life. Neema had worked hard and her hard work paid off; she was so happy. As we mentioned earlier, only this was because she was the only girl from her school at that particular time. More important to Neema was that all the people in her life were happy about her achievement. We told Neema that we were proud of her, and we will continue to celebrate this historical event in our family as long as we live. Neema would just laugh and then she would go and get Michael and she would tell him about what we had just told her. Neema was going to join other girls from all parts of Kenya, from private primary schools and government primary schools.

All the girls would come to learn and understand that they had come to congregate together and they had walked the same road to get there. We still remember Neema telling us that it was scary and thrilling at the same time, just knowing that she passed her standard eight final examinations and the results had indicated that she had met the requirement, and she was good to go. Then she saw herself lifting up her hand for high fives, saying, "I did it."

Neema did it well, as well as the other girls who were joining her. It was a big moment for our daughter Neema to celebrate, a big moment for us as parents, and a big moment as well as challenge for Neema's younger brother Michael. Neema saw one challenge in this new move and she told us that she was looking forward to adjusting and learning to go to school in a girls' boarding environment. She would laugh and tell us that she was looking forward to enjoying this experience as well, because it was going to be different and because she was coming from a mixed boarding school. Michael saw this moment as the most perfect moment it could be, because he stood up and told us that he was not afraid because he knew for sure that he was the next one. Michael made us laugh more because it was so fun watching our two children in this way, and we really enjoyed it.

We were happy to take our new challenge, and we supported Neema in every move until she got settled into her new school. With time we came to learn more about the school Neema went to, the national secondary school. The national secondary school Neema went to after completing her primary school level at standard eight was one of the most famous national secondary schools.

This school was a well-known national secondary school in Kenya because of its reputation in the country, because a good number of famous female politicians attended that school. We still remember the names of those female politicians because Neema had told us about them. Neema told us that the national secondary school she was attending has a good reputation in Kenya, and a lot of parents who had their girls schooling there spoke well of this school. We enjoyed this perspective and understanding, and as parents we continued to be proud of our daughter. So far, Neema was using her voice in a unique way, and we told her that we could hear her and her tone of voice. In a different way, Neema was telling us to just wait and see and watch her, and keep watching her, because she was going to set herself on a journey of becoming another famous young woman like them.

We were not surprised by this because the tone of voice from Neema clearly said it all, that the school itself and its name was already an inspirational setting. Neema was going to make use of this inspirational environment and national secondary school. It was a perfect moment for her because this was a secondary education level with lots of learning, experiments, practice and challenges. Above all, it was the perfect environment to grow up and become a young woman, make friends and continue her education journey and its adventure and have fun. Neema took her new journey seriously, and she did it well. It was at this secondary school where Neema started creating her own unique lifestyle. She was not shy in starting, showing the world the real values of who she was. More important to us was that we began to see our Neema clearly, that she was showing herself to the world, showing what a young woman she was, what she believed as a young woman, what she loved and enjoyed doing. She began to show the world around her what she truly loved, her love for nature, and the work she was doing would always be something to connect her with nature. Neema told us that reading gave her true pleasure and peace.

Neema enjoyed her time at the secondary school she went to, and she made the most of it. More important to us is that she enjoyed everything she was doing, and loved everything, and that she was able to make friends, and she made a good number of them. She would come home to tell us that she was enjoying her new life at secondary school and she was having lots of fun. She was also able to show her teachers and was not shy in letting them know her love for nature as well as her newly developed interest. Neema began to be more interested in reading; we knew our daughter loved to read and that she was reading anything from the day she knew how to read, but this time around it was different because Neema was deeply in love with reading, especially reading novels. Neema loved to read and she would combine her love for nature and her love for reading. Neema would go out around the school garden and sit anywhere where she could experience the beauty and enjoy the natural environment, and she would take a book to read. Neema would read books about all the subjects she was taking at school, but she was particularly interested in novels.

Neema read novels all the time she was not directly involved with the school activities and studying.

Here she got into terrible trouble, because with time she fell in love with novels and she was reading them obsessively in the school environment. Neema being Neema, she was not shy here as well about telling everyone at school, to show them her love for reading novels. Her favorite author was Danielle Steel. Neema was one of the few people on Earth who have read almost all the books written by Danielle Steel at that particular time. She enjoyed and told us about it, she even told her friends at school as well as her friends at home. With time, Neema was overdoing this and we may say that she was obsessed with Danielle Steel's novels. She was still at secondary school at that particular time and her teachers saw what was happening and started to worry about it. Neema was required to remember that she was still a secondary school girl and that she had more work to do to pass her form-four final examinations for her own benefit as well as the secondary school's reputation.

It was obvious to everyone and all the students in her classroom, and all the students in the school, for that matter, as they were required to study and work hard and get good results. The importance of their performance was that good results would take them to the university level and bring the school's name to the top. Teachers did their part, they worked hard to teach and to provide a supportive environment to all the girls, because they wanted them to pass their final form-four examinations. From time to time, teachers would remind all the girls to remember clearly why there were there, and therefore they were required to study and study. Teachers also reminded Neema about studying hard in order to perform well. The teachers become aware of Neema's obsessive habit of reading novels, and they brought this to the attention of the headmistress.

The headmistress called Neema to the office and spoke with her and asked her to cut down novels and concentrate on school subjects. The headmistress and her assistant were on top of the school performance and that meant that they stayed focused and made sure that their school would continue to be one of the top schools in national school secondary final examination results in Kenya. They set achievable goals and worked hard, and invited other stakeholders, including parents of those girls attending that particular secondary school at that particular time, to get involved.

The school board was doing an incredible job on their part, too; they would add to the parents' meeting agenda about the girls, performance, about an individual girls' performance, as well as the meaning of that performance to the school itself. Occasionally, the headmistress and her assistant would conduct one-on-one meetings with parents when deemed necessary. We still remember very well that we were listed for a one-on-one meeting with the headmistress and her assistant. We cooperated and attended the meeting, and we weren't sure what to expect. We had been following up about how Neema was doing at her secondary school level, because we wanted to see Neema do well, pass her form-four final examination and go to university.

Neema was doing well and we were pleased about that as parents, but our minds were unsettled because we were not sure what was going to be said about our girl Neema. Then the headmistress broke the news and told us that she decided to call us because she was worried about Neema's habit of reading novels obsessively. She asked us to tell her about this issue, and said that she wanted us to help Neema because, although she was one of few students doing well, things may change because of the distraction she was creating around herself. The headmistress insisted that she did not want to lose Neema and wanted her to continue to perform well. She was calling for parents' support, and in that way she wanted to help Neema to stay on the right track, stay focused, so her final results would be great.

We thanked the headmistress and her assistant for helping us and promised them that we would work on that and we would help Neema. We went to see Neema and we had a discussion about her love of reading novels, and we asked her to cut down reading novels and wait until after she finished her form-four final examinations. We told Neema exactly what we were told at the parents' meeting, as well as what the headmistress and her assistant had told us. They emphasised individual performance, meaning Neema's performance, and that the individual performance was significantly important to the school's performance. At the end of the day, we all knew that the school in general would get a good record and reputation.

We reminded Neema about this because we wanted her to continue doing well and celebrate her achievements, and the three of us would join her in celebrating as well. Michael too would follow and copy what Neema had done, and above all she was the one who once told us about the school's reputation and its name as well. So, we told Neema that we had agreed with her headmistress and her assistant about one thing, that we were not going to stop Neema from reading novels, and we didn't want to take away her love for reading, but we would like to see her reading very little and increasing her attention to academic reading and books. We also said to Neema, "In short, your headmistress wants us to help you work on finding a good balance and prioritize your reading while you're in the school environment," and we suggested a few things to help her adjust and find a good balance in terms of reading novels and academic books as well as academic materials. Neema listened to what we told her and promised to do better, and that she would follow our suggestions and make sure that her parents don't go to another one-on-one meeting again. We had a happy ending and our meeting with her was an extraordinary experience we will live to remember. Neema apologized and promised us that she was going to do the right thing. We also suggested to her that she should go to the headmistress to apologize, and also find her assistant and apologize as well, and thank them, too.

We went back to the headmistress's office to say goodbye, and we thanked the headmistress again for being honest about our daughter Neema's habit of reading novels obsessively, and we told her about how Neema promised us that she was going to do the right thing and that we would be making a follow-up. We went home satisfied, and the next time we came back to the meeting we saw the headmistress and she told us that Neema was doing well, and she made a follow-up to her teachers and she was told that everything was going well, and that she also spoke with Neema herself, and she told her she was getting better at working and focusing on school subjects. We were happy to hear the good news about our Neema. After our meeting we went to see Neema, and we told her that her teachers and especially her headmistress were pleased to see her adjusting and getting better. Neema told us that she took the suggestions both from us and from her teachers seriously, because she wanted to pass her form-four final examinations and she wanted to go to university.

Neema completed her form-four and did her final examinations as required at secondary school level and graduated. After her graduation she set herself free and took a little break, waiting for her final form-four national examination results. She went home to wait for the results and told us that she was optimistic and hoped that she was going to pass her final examinations, and would break the record because she believed in herself. She even remembered about the one-on-one meeting we had with the headmistress and her assistant about her reading novels obsessively at school. It was a beautiful memory, because Neema accepted that that particular meeting was a wake-up call to her, and that she would live to remember it. And she said, "I worked hard and pulled up my socks, and I believe in myself and in what I have done, and I want my headmistress and her assistant to be happy about my results. More important to me is that I want my parents to be happy and I also want my school to get a good record and reputation. I don't want to forget my young brother Michael; I want him to see my performance. I would like to see myself leaving behind a good record, same as those famous female politicians in Kenya who attended the same national secondary school."

Chapter Four

2007-2011

By the time Neema completed her secondary school in Kenya, we were in London, England. Neema came to London to live with us and stayed with us and waited for her secondary school final examination results to come out. She was happy to take a break for a couple of months. More important to her was that she would be away from academic books and therefore she could continue reading her novels.

She enjoyed London, and sometimes joked about being on an adventure and exploring the famous city, one of the most popular and beautiful cities on Earth. The time came, and Neema got her form-four final results, and she was happy that she did well, and her pass mark meant that she qualified for university entry. Again, we were there for her, congratulated her, told her that we continued to be proud of her and what she had done so far. We also thanked her for setting an example for Michael to follow in the future. Neema was so happy again, and she started searching right away, looking for university programs suitable for her. She told us that she was looking for programs to continue her interest and her love for nature and her love for reading. We remember her saying that she was looking to apply for something similar to what she loved and enjoyed doing. We did not want to guess the answer to our question, and we decided to ask her what she was going to do. Neema laughed first and then said, "The same. I am going to continue to build what I started to love, enjoy doing and always be happy to do it."

Neema told us that she would like to search, apply and study something related to nature and reading. We definitely knew that Neema would go and continue to grow and keep on building her love for nature and her love for reading. We were not surprised about this answer because we had been watching Neema show us her love for nature and her love for reading. We remembered her obsessive reading of novels and the way she would tell people in her life cycle that reading was something important for her, because reading was giving her pleasure and a sense of peace. Although, at that particular time, we were not sure if Neema would go and pick one of the two or she would just find something with the opportunity to combine the two together, but we clearly saw her career and direction.

Neema searched and searched and went and applied for a TV broadcasting course. She told us she had chosen that course because it was fitting well with her passion. Her love for nature and her love for reading would fit perfectly and match with this course when she combined both of them together. She also told us that the course she was going to take would give her more opportunities and open more doors for her to learn more about the world around her, especially nature, and on top of that more travelling and meeting new people and new cultures.

She was very thrilled about going to university to do this course and told us that she was looking forward to having a lot of fun, going on adventures and exploring the world and the people who would become her audience, and she would be able to learn more from them and understand how they treat nature around them. Of course, she would get the opportunity to continue her reading habit to help her gain an understanding of her audience in terms of their culture, languages and their way of living before travelling to their land and environment.

As we write this book today, it was as if the university requirements read her mind, and when the university asked her to provide a piece of writing work as a condition of being accepted, Neema focused on her audience right away and she wrote this article:

A 500-word essay that analyses a recently broadcast television programme that makes imaginative and effective use of sound and image.

The World news presentation was clearly well organised, as is the case with all news items at CNN International. The main topic of discussion was the Queen's visit to the United States of America, which included a live coverage of the events that were unfolding at the White House's premises where the Queen was meeting the President of the United States of America.

It all started at a good note and with perfect organisation, the presenter at the studio and the one stationed at the premises of the White House all started off well with each one of them giving a brief introduction of how they were going to cover the event live. This introduction was presented eloquently and enabled the viewers (even those who had no

idea of what was about to happen) to understand what was going to take place and anticipated for the event.

The presenters also did not fall short of making the presentation alive and they achieved this by adding in bits of information that was interesting as well as educating, most of the time informing people of interesting bits about the Royal Family. In fact they achieved to present the live coverage as much of an interesting piece of program rather than news.

It was verging on the informal, an aspect in which most viewers are willing to endure as entertainment. This was a good way for them to break the monotony of news articles, that at most times appeals only to the middle aged and older generation.

The order in which the various events were presented was clearly well arranged in a sequential order. The order was in a way that the presenters in the studio gave their views or comments on certain events that have been seen or are just about to be seen. This is then followed by the comments or the views of the presenter at the premises of the event. This was a good way of making sure that the viewers understood every image that was being shown and followed everything said with the appropriate action. This enabled a smooth and clear flow of the whole broadcast. This kind of presentation, one that incorporated good presentation of events and the explanation of events enabled the viewers to understand what was happening and clearly also helped to provide for good entertainment.

However, although it was a good presentation the program did not give the viewers a long period of viewing the images and after the first events all the other events were not featured (i.e. the events that took place later on after the public appearance of the two leaders). In most cases the presenters had to interrupt the viewing of the images on the screen by giving details and explaining what was actually happening for rather long periods of time and although this created suspense, it was a rather long wait for viewers who were keen to see what was actually happening.

The flow of the presentation was also interrupted by the frequent loss of sound and at the place where the live events were taking place and although this quickly fixed, proved to be something that altered the people's view of the program. Most viewers found that although these problems occurred, they were not enough factors to prevent them from viewing the program, and hence at the end the entire program managed to pull many viewers and reached its targeted audience. All the good presentations overshadowed the mishaps, so all in all it proved to be good and entertaining viewing for audiences of all ages and all walks of life, and it proved to also be educative in nature as it provided adequate and detailed information of the Royal Family that most people (especially outside the United Kingdom) did not know about.

Neema Edward Mkwelele
BA (Hons) Broadcasting at University College Falmouth

At the end of this, Neema accepted the offer she was given by the University of Falmouth in Cornwall in the southwest and south coast of England.

She went to live there and enjoyed travelling through other parts of southwest England like Exeter and Plymouth.

She told us about her university and the people of Cornwall, and she generally enjoyed everything. More important to Neema was that she began to fall in love with Cornwall. Neema enjoyed her school life in the Cornwall area at the University of Falmouth. She would write to us, send us photographs of the university and the area itself, the beauty and especially the beautiful beaches of the south coast of England. Cornwall is a beautiful place to live, that's what Neema would tell us, tell her brother Michael, and tell her friends and everyone in her life cycle.

Here is Neema relaxing and enjoying the beaches of southeast England in beautiful Cornwall.

She would go and post on her Twitter account and say, "Neema lives in a beautiful Cornwall." So, she wanted the world to hear her tone when she was saying that Cornwall is one of the most beautiful places in the world, and that she was referring to her own perspectives and her values. It was because of who she was, the person Neema grew up to become, and her unique way of looking at her life and understanding the world around her. More important to us is that it was about values, that Neema and her values and her own way of showing the world who she was. It was her way of showing the world that she was enjoying what she was doing as well as loving everything she was doing and experiencing, and in particular her love for nature and her love for reading.

Neema was happy to share with us and the whole world about her experience as well as about what she truly believed and what made her the person she was. She was a unique, very smart person, creative and curious and willing to do whatever it took to learn and educate herself as well as others. Neema would work and use resources around her in order to enjoy what she loved doing. She would always say, "I want a simple life, and I will use anything around me to help me do what I enjoy and love doing." She would insist that nature was something she would always turn to because it was always available with no cost.

We still remember one of her photographs showing Neema at the beach, a Cornwall beach with lots of rocks. In that photograph we saw Neema refusing to allow those rocks at the beach to take the pleasure of reading her book away. At that particular time Neema had her beach towel and a book, and she decided to lay her towel down on top of the rocks and place the book on top of her towel, and she started to read comfortably. It was amazing to see how creative our daughter Neema had become; in the end she had peace of mind because she created her own world using only the resources around her. It was that particular time that we understood Neema's ability, that she was able to combine her love for nature and her love for reading to make her life simple, and to continue doing what she loved doing, and the combination worked perfectly for her. More important to us is that this one experience alone is part of the inspirational story about Neema, and we continue to be proud of her.

Here Neema is using her own personal bath towel to comfortably enjoy reading her book. The message is clear that she was one of those people who would go out and do their best to be happy because they love what they do in their lives. Neema put her towel down to cover rocks and enjoy reading her book. We kept her towel for our own beautiful memory about her.

Neema did not forget her young brother Michael. She continued to communicate with Michael in Kenya. She told us that she would be happy to see Michael visiting her in Cornwall at the University of Falmouth. This was because Neema came to London to join us alone and left her young brother Michael in Kenya. Michael was doing his secondary school, and he was required to stay behind to complete his form four the same way his sister did. We were allowed ask for a transfer to take Michael to London and we decided not to do that. We were comfortable with the education plan we created for Neema and Michael and therefore we wanted our two children to take the plan we had created for them. We spoke with them and explained to them that because Neema and Michael were by then old enough to contribute to their own wellbeing, and they understood this, it was the way it was, and Michael was left behind. Michael was happy to stay behind and complete his secondary school because he too did well on his standard-eight examinations and he was one of the few students who went to number-one-category secondary schools in Kenya like his sister Neema. It was not hard for him because he was allowed to come to London during his school vacation to join his parents and his sister. Michael came to London, and he was also able to travel to Cornwall to visit his sister at the University of Falmouth as well.

The two of them enjoyed getting together again and getting an opportunity to spend quality time together. More important for both of them was that Michael was able to see how his sister was doing and making out at the university. And it was an important time for Neema to be able to share with her brother her story about studying at the university, her life in general and the beautiful place she was living. She was happy to show her brother around and take him to the university building and she also took him to one of the beautiful beaches on the southwest coast of England. Michael enjoyed the visit and loved everything. In the end both shared among themselves how life was treating them on both sides. Michael came back to London to tell us about what he saw and about his experience. He would also come to see that it was an enjoyable trip he had made in his life, and he dreamt for more to come.

As we write this book we continue to be proud of our children and we continue to be proud of our daughter Neema. We always remind ourselves about the special gift and we think about those precious moment and beautiful memories Neema left behind.

She was a fun girl to be around.

Neema continued to stay in Cornwall and was doing well with studies at the University of Falmouth. She enjoyed her time and everything around her, made friends, attended various activities at the university, including partying as much as she could have done.

What is more important to us is that those precious moments and beautiful memories Neema left behind would not only be for us to enjoy and treasure but would be there for her young brother Michael and the whole world to join us and celebrate her short life.

She also found herself having a stable relationship.

Relationships were something important for Neema. We're writing to speak on behalf of Neema and happy to share with you that we agree with our late Neema that relationships are important in our lives and something important for our happiness.

In January 2009, on her second year at the University of Falmouth, Neema was shortlisted to be one of the few students selected to travel outside England for an international exchange program. She was one of those students who would travel to Vancouver, Canada. The Emily Carr University in Vancouver accepted Neema to be one of their international exchange students. The program was planned well and prepared by the international student officer at the University of Falmouth. The international student's officer at Falmouth University arranged and worked with Emily Carr University on behalf of Neema.

Neema was so happy and excited at the same time. She came to London to tell us about her trip. She also came to London to work on getting a Canadian student visa. We worked with her and helped her to get a student visa from the Canadian High Commission in London to allow her to enter Canada as an international exchange student. When her departure date came we took Neema to the airport. Neema took British Airways from London Heathrow airport to Vancouver airport. We still remember until today how excited she was when we took her to the airport. She went to check in at London Heathrow terminal five and enjoyed excellent light. At that particular time, terminal five was designated as the terminal for British Airways only, both inbound and outbound, that alone meant a lot to Neema. We still remember her saying, "What a wonderful experience, and I am enjoying every moment."

Neema was one of the passengers travelling with British Airways from London to Vancouver. As one of the outbound passengers she was excited because it was exciting to all passengers, and Neema found herself being one of them. On arrival at Vancouver Airport, Neema sent us an email and told us that she arrived safely in Vancouver. She also promised to write later on and that she would write more. We can still hear the tone of her excitement, even from her writing. We couldn't wait for her to get access to a telephone so we could hear her excited voice. It was really a big thing to her and more importantly to us—it was a big thing to us as a family. Neema was the first person from our entire family to put her feet on Canadian soil as well as the first family member to go to North America. We would come to learn that Neema made a big accomplishment in terms of travelling, and she made her own history and left that history behind. We were proud of her and we continue to be proud of her and we are happy to share with the world those happy moments Neema had enjoyed and all beautiful memories she left behind.

Neema liked the Vancouver city and enjoyed her life in Vancouver and she stayed very close to Emily Carr University. She stayed at Emily Carr as an international exchange student for six months only. She then left to go back to England and continue her studies. She came back to London with lots of photographs and stories to tell us. We enjoyed listening to Neema tell us about her travelling experiences and her love for the beauty of British Columbia. We enjoyed seeing that Neema was busy, not only with the studies but when she was out and about, and we especially enjoyed looking at the beautiful parks in Metro Vancouver that Neema visited and hung out in with classmates or friends.

Neema told us that she enjoyed experiencing the beauty of British Columbia and loved everything. At one point Neema found herself comparing the beauty she was experiencing in Canada with the beauty she left behind in Cornwall at the University of Falmouth. She told us that although she was in Vancouver for only six months, the time was good enough for her to see and experience its beauty and nature. Neema continued to tell us that Metro Vancouver and its cities are beautiful, and so is British Columbia, but Cornwall was still the most beautiful place on Earth, according to her. Neema was not shy about persuading us to move to Canada, and she would tell us that Canada is a one of the most beautiful countries on Earth and maybe we should consider moving there. In the beginning we thought that Neema was trying to talk to us about it because she was just excited, and she was still excited and wanted to continue to show us her love for nature. We also thought that Neema herself was about to tell us that she was considering moving to Canada because she wanted to see herself going back to Canada again to visit and enjoy the beauty she left behind. We were wrong, Neema was actually serious, and she meant everything she said about us considering a move to Canada.

Neema went back to Cornwall to continue her studies at the University of Falmouth. While she was still in Cornwall at the University of Falmouth, Neema wrote to us about her trip to Vancouver, Canada. She wrote and added more photographs and reminded us about what she said the day she came back from Vancouver. She would finish writing by saying, "I want you guys to think about it, because Vancouver is beautiful."

Then one day she told us that she was enjoying Cornwall because it is a beautiful place on Earth, like Vancouver, but the beauty she experienced in Vancouver, British Columbia is different from what she was experiencing in Cornwall, England. We appreciated our daughter Neema's attitude and we told her that we will continue to be proud of her as long as we live, and therefore we promised her that we would like to take time to think about it. We also told her that we were enjoying hearing from her and happy to listen to what she told us about her travelling experience and what it means to live in one of the most beautiful places on Earth.

Chapter Five

Searching for flowers has special meaning to our late daughter Neema. It has special meaning to us because we're so proud of her, and we continue to be proud of her.

Neema's death at a very young age taught us a lot of things, we can learn now that the exposure we provided to her was incredibly amazing; she engulfed herself in her own world, in the nature, loved the nature and made the best use of it. Neema quickly learned to love and enjoy nature in her own unique way, and creatively she would combine her love for nature with other interests she grew to develop, things like her love for reading.

Searching for flowers has special meaning
to our late daughter Neema.

We're sharing with you what our late daughter Neema taught us and also what she shared with us in her very short life. Her love for nature was something very important for her as well as her love for reading; they contributed to Neema's life and excitement. Neema was excited about the nature around her and the beauty of nature she was experiencing. She lived and did her best to appreciate life and especially nature and the beauty that nature brought with it and anything about nature in her life cycle and around her. She wanted to live a simple life. We watched her and we enjoyed hearing her voice, her love for nature in every action and move. She lived by the flowers, she was a flower.

Neema shared with insects around her as
well, more than just living by flower.

Neema worked very hard and engaged herself with knowledge
and understanding about how to broadcast her love for nature
and how she lived to love the beauty and nature around her.
For Neema, it was all about the act of living and enjoying the
moments of life, in particular the moments when nature brings
beauty around you to enjoy. Making life less complicated was
very important to her, and she was always happy to tell people
about it or just speak by action by wearing flowers on her feet.
She would for example sometimes call it a game. Most of the
time she was referring to reading and that was like a game to
Neema. Neema would say, "Reading is a great game and a great
pleasure"—this was what she told people about her age and her
challenges, and how her way of searching hope and happiness
meant a lot to her, and therefore finding such a treasure would
surely bring her joy. Neema would say, "I read books, and read
and read because reading means a great deal to me."

The reason for this book is to tell about Neema, and we're happy
to share with you and the world these beautiful memories that
Neema left behind. What's more important to us is that we
continue to be proud of her and continue to be proud of everything
she did, and we continue to be proud of her accomplishments at
a very young age. What Neema left behind has become a legacy,

and we have decided to share with the world Neema's legacy and we will carry this legacy with us because Neema is not with us to speak for herself and tell the world who she was, what her unique values were and what she would like other young women of her age to learn from her. We also believe that other girls and young women of her age would be inspired to follow Neema's footsteps, and although Neema is not around on Earth to get those girls to connect with her, we're optimistic that this book and the story about Neema will be good enough for other girls and the world to connect with Neema and her values.

Who was Neema? This is an inspirational story for all girls and young women under twenty-five years of age from all backgrounds to read. We hope all girls go out and read this book and then after reading this book will agree with us. We also hope that all people around the world who go out and read this book will agree with us, and therefore we're optimistic that all people around the world will begin to help girls and women, working together to support those girls and young women in their journey of searching for their own favourite flowers, and find their own ways to broadcast them to the world. We have learned this from Neema, that this is a unique way for girls and young women of Neema's age to voice loudly and tell the world that they do exist. We're looking forward to seeing many girls and young women searching for their favourite flowers because there are beautiful flowers out there for those who want to see them. We will be happy to be one of their audiences one day, the same way we were for our Neema.

Telling the world about Neema and all the beautiful memories she left behind is our way of telling the world where we are now in our journey, our special grieving journey. We continue to honour our beautiful daughter, we continue to be proud of her and we continue to share the beautiful memories she left behind. We carry on those memories carefully because we are carrying her legacy and we want to share this legacy with all people on Earth because we loved her dearly and we will always love her. We also believe in sharing good things with other people in life, and therefore anything good coming out of the short life of Neema would be good to all girls and young women of her age on Earth. We're proud to say that it is beautiful and worth doing.

Writing this book is important to us because we want to use this opportunity to give back to the world at all levels and to all people. The great support we have received and are still receiving after we lost Neema has contributed to change and shaped us because we now know who we are, who we have become and we have discovered our purpose in life, our new life without Neema being with us on Earth. We have gone deeply into ourselves and have deep connections with our values. We have decided to immerse ourselves in our gratitude. And we appreciate the fact that we're blessed with the special gift of being Neema's parents. And Michael is blessed to be Neema's young brother. We have enjoyed the very short life Neema had on Earth and with us.

We will live to remember that the beauty of Neema's values is a legacy. Neema's legacy was left behind to us, and it is an inspiration to all people around the world, and in particular girls and young women of Neema's age. We continue to say that we wrote this book because we also believe from the bottom of our hearts that this is what Neema would like to see happening. She would have wanted the world to see her wearing flowers on her feet and she would also have wanted the world to hear her voice from walking with the flowers.

Neema would have wanted the world to hear the voice of children and young people, and in particular girls and young women around the world, the sound when they walk wearing their beautiful flowers on their feet. Meaning that those girls and young women around the world have worked hard in the same way Neema did, searching for their favourite flowers, and they were able to see them and finally find their ways to broadcast them, and therefore find their unique values. This is what Neema would have wanted the world to hear from children and young people, to say that they will go out and ask for help and support, and that they will wear flowers on their feet because they worked hard to get them, and therefore they can now see themselves, and the walk by itself is a voice and a cry for help and they are saying help us because we would like to contribute to the world and we're ready and we know what we love and what we want to do and what we're loving doing and we just want opportunities to let us equip ourselves with knowledge and skills, then we will all be ready and set to contribute to the world we live in our own unique way happily.

She worked hard, thrilled and excelled, and she called herself "Unbroken Divine," she graduated with BA Honours in Broadcasting. Neema was ready to contribute to the world. "I worked in the international office at Falmouth University. I worked with Neema when she came to Falmouth University. She was a wonderful person who received one of the very few scholarships as an outstanding student. I also worked with her to set up her study abroad in Canada, where Neema again made a big impression. I am sorry to hear of her passing and her loss to you, her family, and wider world of such a beautiful and talented person." (2011) A quote from Stuart Westhead, an international student officer from Falmouth University, United Kingdom.

We believe that Neema lived by her values, "lived by flowers," and more important to us is that we're happy to tell the world that she not only lived by flowers but she also walked by flowers as her way of sharing with the world and telling everyone around her that she was telling what kind of person she was.

Neema was carefully picking up her favourite
flowers to wear on her feet and broadcast the
love of what she loved to do in her life.

Flowers are everywhere for those who want to see them.

Neema's smiles tell it all: that she was ready
and set and going to search for flowers.

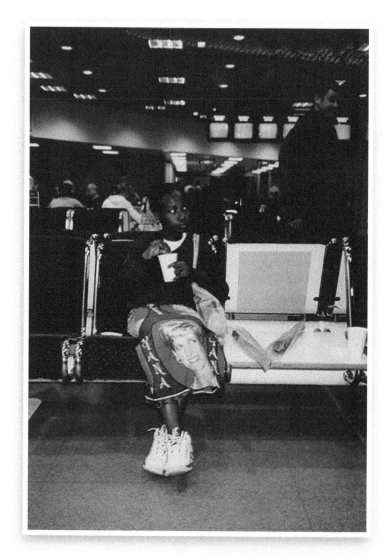

Neema was fond of Diana, Princess of Wales.

Neema

Bertha Mkwelele and Edward Mkwelele are co-founders of Neema Edward Mkwelele Wellness Foundation.

Visit www.neemaedwardmkwelelewellnessfoundation.org